JIM ARNOSKY

FOLLOWING the COAST

HarperCollinsPublishers

Following the Coast
Copyright © 2004 by Jim Arnosky
Manufactured in China by South China Printing Company Ltd.
All rights reserved.
www.harperchildrens.com

Library of Congress Cataloging-in-Publication Data
Arnosky, Jim.
Following the coast / Jim Arnosky.—1st ed.
p.   cm.
Summary: On their travels up the East Coast,
the author and his wife describe the wildlife they
encounter in different salt marshes.
ISBN 0-688-17117-6. — ISBN 0-688-17118-4
(lib. bdg.)
1. Salt marsh animals—Atlantic Coast (U.S.)—
Juvenile literature. [1. Salt marsh animals.
2. Zoology—Atlantic Coast (U.S.) 3. Atlantic
Coast (U.S.)—Description and travel.] I. Title.
QL157 .A84A75 2004   591.769'0975—dc21
2003009557   CIP
AC

Typography by Stephanie Bart-Horvath
1 2 3 4 5 6 7 8 9 10
❖
First Edition

Deanna and I dedicate this book
to our three grandsons,
Darren, Derek, and Conner.

*Tide returning,
Jekyll Island, Georgia*

INTRODUCTION

LIKE WATERBIRDS HEADING NORTH in spring, my wife, Deanna, and I followed the coastal marshes from Florida's Banana River to Bombay Hook on the Delaware shore. As we discovered miles of picturesque seaside roads, our minds gathered in scenes of creeks, bays, boats, lighthouses, and towns.

With camera and sketchbook, we recorded a collage of moments and memories to share with you. This salt marsh album was written to ebb and flow like the tide. Look long at the pages. Let the words and pictures be your dream of someday —all grown-up and on your own— happily, slowly, lazily following the coast.

Jim Arnosky
Crinkle Cove

*Florida manatees
Indian River Lagoon*

*White pelicans on a sandbar.
The white pelican is the largest bird
in North America.*

WE WANTED TO SEE the white pelicans that fish the sparkling waters around Florida's Cape Canaveral. That simple desire to watch big beautiful birds gave us the perfect starting point for our salt marsh journey. We also saw fourteen manatees! Youngsters and adults were all huddling together in a lagoon. The rivers and streams in this northernmost portion of their range were becoming cool, and manatees need to stay warm. We watched until the group swam slowly away, heading south to warmer water. Deanna and I waved good-bye. Our compass was pointing north.

We followed the coast northward, finding salt
marshes all along the way, stopping every so often
to watch the rich variety of waterbirds a salt marsh
can attract. We found that the very best time to
see waterbirds is at low tide, when all of the food
in the marsh becomes easier to find. Wading
birds, such as these roseate spoonbills,
fly in to feast on crabs and mollusks living
in the mud and shallow pools.

To be in a salt marsh at low tide at sundown is an experience that pleases all the senses. Tidal land oozes under your step. The sky shimmers with color. The air smells of salt, seaweeds, and mud. Small birds and gentle breezes rustle the tall grass. And fishing boats chug along, slowly finding their way home through a maze of narrow channels.

When the tide comes in, the flood of water stirs the marsh bottom, making it murky with the microscopic foods that crabs, shellfish, and shrimp thrive on. One beautiful Georgia morning we were watching a shrimp boat working the water on the edge of a large salt marsh. In the boat's wake dolphins were chasing fish that had escaped the shrimper's nets. The dolphins looked very black against the blue water, and I began sketching them with pen-and-ink. While I sketched, Deanna visited a nearby lighthouse and, finding it open to the public, climbed its spiral staircase to the top.

Dolphins surfacing— one, two . . .

three in a row!

This dolphin tail came up slowly, moving like a tiny whale tail.

Five dolphins chasing fish in close quarters, gulls hovering on the alert for any pieces of chomped-up fish

Banded water snake on a dock

Cottonmouth moccasin

Anywhere you see trees growing
in a marsh, there are small
islands that snakes can coil on.

In case you were wondering—there
are snakes in the coastal marshes.
Nonvenomous water snakes and dangerous
venomous moccasins and rattlers inhabit
the grassy shores, mud banks, freshwater
streams, and wooded islands. Our largest
venomous snake, the eastern diamondback
rattlesnake, is a powerful swimmer. Diamondbacks
have been seen swimming in the surf, migrating from
one offshore island to another. Deanna and I watch for
snakes wherever there is water, tall grass, and mud or a
beached boat where a snake can be coiled in the sun or
hiding in the shade.

*Water snake climbing
to sun itself on a b*

Tides are caused by the gravitational pull of the sun and moon on the earth's surface. Low tide occurs when the pull is most powerful, causing the ocean to bulge upward and draw water away from the land.

High tide happens when the gravitational pull weakens and ocean water can flow more freely toward the shore. There are two high tides and two low tides every day.

MOLLY DEAR
S.C.

Coastal people know the timing of the tides and take advantage of them for fishing, crabbing, oystering, and clamming. Simple plywood fishing boats like this one are left to rise and fall with the tides until they are needed. And when the owner of the boat is not around, the wildlife makes good use of it.

This is one of my favorite birds. Its official name is northern harrier, but I prefer to call it a marsh hawk because I've seen it in southern as well as northern marshes.

Look closely at the grass in a salt marsh and you will see small snails climbing up and down the blades. These periwinkle snails are shown two times their actual size.

In a salt marsh any quick movement you notice on mud or wet sand might be that of a fiddler crab. Fiddler crabs are named for their single large fighting claw

We have a system for locating wildlife in a marsh. Using binoculars, we scan the tops of the grasses for birds flying low. Then we search the grass blades, looking for hidden birds, nests, spiders, webs, or snails. Lastly we zero in on the sand or mud, focusing on the movements of clams or crabs.

Deanna is the quicker to spot animals. Whenever I'm researching a particular species, she often finds it before I do and needles me by saying, "I win!"

While I am busy making field sketches like these two of fishing boats, Deanna is looking for wildlife hidden in the scenery.

Here she is with her trusty binoculars.

White marlin

Right whale

The meandering channels and creeks in a salt marsh are sheltered from wind and waves by the tall grass blades. Within the marsh all is calm. It's hard to remember that the tide inching in is part of the ocean's thousands of miles of distance and depth.

The saltwater slowly flooding a salt marsh is the same water in which the world's largest and most powerful creatures freely swim. All of them depend on the protected waters of coastal marshes. The marsh provides breeding areas where their young can develop and grow strong enough to live in the sea. And it produces the billions of shrimp and other small but important marine creatures at the bottom of the food chain.

*Manta ray
and bull shark*

Deer hoofprints
on a barrier island beach

Where there are bears, they stay close to the lowland woods.

Deer venture from the woods to the marshes and on to the barrier island beaches.

Raccoons are everywhere.

The channels that separate barrier islands from salt marshes provide protected waterways for boats cruising north and south along the coast.

In many places along the coast, the sheltered waters of salt marshes are further protected from the power of the sea by long narrow nearshore islands. Protected by these barrier islands, mainland trees can grow tall. Grasses give way to brush, and woodland plants take hold. Where there are barrier islands, some extensive coastal forests have grown up. Near these lowland forests, raccoons, deer, and bear can sometimes be seen wading in the salt marsh, swimming across deep channels, and even walking on the barrier island beaches.

When we reached the barrier islands of North Carolina, the weather turned cold and blustery. Deanna and I were looking out over a windswept marsh when I spotted an animal swimming toward us. It resembled a muskrat. Suddenly I realized I was looking at a nutria! Nutria are aquatic rodents related to muskrats and beavers. Native to South America and introduced in the waters of

Louisiana in 1900, nutria have been spreading northward along the coast ever since. In some places along the coast where migrating nutria have overpopulated the marshland, they are looked on as unwelcome intruders. But to Deanna and me, the three nutria we saw swimming at sunset seemed right at home.

A nutria's long walruslike whiskers can be seen best when the animal is out of the water.

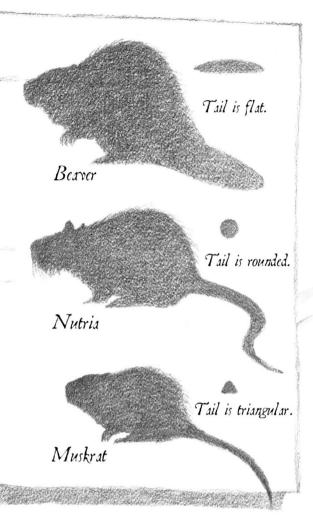

Beaver — Tail is flat.

Nutria — Tail is rounded.

Muskrat — Tail is triangular.

The chart above shows the sizes of a beaver, nutria, and muskrat in proportion to one another.

The nutria shown here actual size is the one I videotaped at sundown.

We kept moving northward, hugging the coast. In Virginia, at the edge of a broad, sun-drenched salt marsh, I saw this fishing trawler propped up out of the water and freshly painted. Sturdy old boats like this are prized and never retired. They work and work. They get painted and repainted, repaired and overhauled, and they work some more.

We left the old boat and, following the narrow road along the edge of the marsh, we crossed over a small bridge to an island called Assateague. Assateague Island is inhabited only by birds, deer, raccoons, and a very special herd of wild ponies. Nobody knows how the multicolored ponies originally came to Assateague. Legend has it that hundreds of years ago a Spanish ship wrecked off the coast. Some ponies aboard escaped drowning by swimming to the island, and there have been ponies living wild on Assateague ever since.

While I zoom in on some nearby ponies feeding on the salty grass, Deanna scans the marsh for other ponies that may be headed our way.

Just after sundown the brilliance of the day gone by lingers, shimmering in still water. This is the time I love most—when all of nature seems to rest—when the sound of small hooves gently stepping turns your head and the muffled noise of feathers being ruffled reveals birds' hidden nests.

We were nearing the end of our journey. Home was just a day away. With winter cold and heavy in the night air, Deanna and I said good-bye to Assateague and promised we'd come back.

Canada geese
Bombay Hook, Delaware

Deanna drove across the Delaware state line carrying precious cargo. We had a treasure trove of sights and sounds captured on video. My sketchbook was bulging with over a hundred heavily inked pages of drawings and nature notes. Deanna's laptop computer was loaded with dozens of digital photos. And most precious of all were the many wonderful memories we had of marshes, beaches, and wildlife near the sea. Now our route veered inland, away from the coast, to the snow-covered hills of Vermont. But spring was going our way, flying north on the wings of migrating geese.